Mud Ajar

Mud Ajar

poems

Hiram Larew

atmosphere press

Contents

~ For West Virginia ~

Magic

The stars in your chest --
     the sounds of their glow
     their flash blink wings
     their touch top skies.

These leaps towards light --
     these grateful urging holy stars
     in your chest and now
          in your throat.

Their voices of beams
     that echo into your heart and beyond.

Their blaze --
     each star that sparks inside your chest
     and spins out from there.

Spins you as nothing else can
     as when magic comes true
     both inside and out.

With each and every star
     so over the moon.

Quiets Come

All is up
     yes
     all is sky

All is wings and tops and rise

All is up these branches hum
     and whistles high --
     how quiets come

Or beams of clouds
     this world of still
     that flies towards yes
     and shall --
     above what will and all

Where most of more
     calls glowing

Ode to the Edge

of barley swept brooms
of moons learned and books overgrown
of clamoring salt or silvery youth
    and stems of smoke
    and tables' roots
    or views knotted

of loosened stones
    and rustled sleep
    in nestled flings
of corner tunes and passings told
of borders loved
or lostings in
    and slipping spins

such bracken faith --
    this candled roam
    these light-dimmed rhymes of boyhood
    these limbing downs and haystacks brushed
    this plunge and smear of dawning yawns
        or sunset dreams
    the skyward's blending sounds
        and humming slopes up-tugging
    and spindle stars or crusted homes
    and rounding views of evening
        these odes to edge
            in clouds' full-urging scuttle
            or dinner lights that ramble

such streakling skies --
    all arrows lift their grateful views
        sung-up like curves
    the call of bogs
    where sedge surrounds

where lands fold far beyond
    with knowing wings or ways
where land sees just ahead
    through each and every
    dangle heart

Patio

As they look down into the swaddled bundle
>these parents and grandparents
>in an old snapshot
>seem hushed with time
>in glossy and magical ways.

A door looks to be opening behind them
>and a trellis up over them
>casts shadows
>like grins.

They aren't speaking to each other
>or looking up towards the camera.
They needn't be.
They are in awe of the baby.
The grandfather especially
>must realize that the June air
>is melting away.

Because look how the patio has petunias
>and paper plates floating off
>and even a distant train is whistling
>all with no focus or edges --
>>only remembered.
Some purple martins are surely curling the corners
>somewhere.

So here's the wonder --
>How does anyone ever stay put
>now or then
>when everything matters
>in such long-ago pictures --
>>when summer is posed
>>both for spring and fall?

As Where I Love

Who takes anywhere my love along
  or sallies forth to there and sees
  your ways as much as where I love
    each rucksack view of hillsides

On these roads of send or just arrived
  as visits from my love
  or held inside
    my travels to such new
    and greetings bend

And then the skies where where
    flies back and forth
    to love the air like yes and breeze

With every fresh and fro-ing to --
  that listening leaf
    my hiking heart

Your compass grin and magic wise

How anywhere may wave to dreams
  or know to stay my love
  and then begin again in rustled time --
    out towards your whistling ways
    with birds this keen

Clatter

Love me in the very same way that
    the word *unbeknownst* sounds
    in midair
Yes or
    just like how spires climb to the very top

And then
    even beyond soap's slip
    or noon's drift
        and as far as puddles can jump
Love to love me like that

And love me as if handshakes were grins
    or as when echoes find their tunnel
Love me like those birds that love diving and corners
    or just like sunlight is love
        as it teases the cupboards

Love me in all those ways and more

And with sashes open
Love me now but also then
    and as much as when
        lunch is served
        with all of that back and forth
        and clatter
Yes love me as surely as cups that will spill

Or then above
    with night's excel
    when listening turns to dreams
Love me like the swirling din
    within the word *abound*

Our Us

Dazzle breathe these slanted nights
    with gauzy stars and every most
    as outside ins us
        and so
        shines open over love
        shines reaching
        shines new so back and forth.

Blink true our moon
    that opens eyes
Then look above
    these waking branches
        and so be dawned in fulward.

Then even more
    in majest's more
        make razzle rising ways.

But most of all and over all
    upcaw our bless
        and gleam us.

Radio

That was so long ago that it's hard to even pinch --
Since then whole hills have turned the other way
And most babies from such times have left home
      and come back married
        Yes, trees from back then are now two-by-fours.

So why bother with such things that should be forgotten?
Why let years ago punch me flat?
Why oh why should these all-of-a-sudden sounds
      of a nearly lost song
      spook me?

I'll tell you why --
Because that tune this morning cried out like a ghost
      and slipped me right back to when
      my heart had just barely started.
The croon reached right out and grabbed me by my surelys
      and kicked me flat on my dammits
      kicked me all the way back to those days when
I was fool-smack in love
      like a thrown cursing
      glass of milk.

Achill Sound

When the roads curve like sound
    and dip as if lifting to bow
Whenever all thoughts round or cluster
    or when hearts call down
        is Ireland

And as rich when poor was
    or as wise as bare heads in snow ever seemed
    and as twigs so frail broke into song
    and as true as any blight or potato could be
        was Ireland

So when sand laps the senses
    or salt drips the edges of dreams
Whenever hope streams through such heavens
    and moss comes home
    or hearts beam down
        is Ireland

So What

By the way
In spite of what you've been told
    gradual is *not* always better
    or holy.

Taking things slowly
    a step at a time
    is maybe how mountains rise up
    yes
    or how stars twinkle back.
It may even partly explain worldly progress.

But in the end
    suddenly is ten times wider
    fifty times richer
    and so much more exciting to kiss
        than is caution.

What's all at once
    just makes sense
    right down to its nubs.

It's the truth --
    potatoes crave onions.

And speaking of love --
    How do we turn these best laid plans
        into wild weedy patches?
    How do we stoke up lulling mornings?

Yes at the heart of it all
    slow and balm really don't matter --
The world only spins
    on what's panting.

Since

Memories of you
    from our since then
    end on why
    as if you had been my
    my.

Now your if
    seems as far gone on
    as a why note.

So why is this now
    so nearly lost --
    but you?

Let far say.
Let far see as much
    as these left behind
    might gifts.

Let far be how
    your was
    will always shall me.

An Gorta Mór

Our years are easy now --
 all buy and bake or
 folded warm and savored bright
Our full and hills enjoy flowing-over lives
Our easy goods and glads that sweep ahead
  are of so little wanting

But turning round and turning back we ask
What happened here
 in corners bleak --
  the barely breathing
  the blighted rot
  the blankets' cold unweaving
  and eyes like cries inside the hearts
   the digging bells
   these sweeps of death
   and shrouded blame
   all left behind
    poor cherished

Yes, what of An Gorta Mór --
 our vision smudged
 our stories begged
 our grasses' grave
 this unholy shame
  those digging bells

And so when we lean out sills of plenty now
  with freshing paint
  to look ahead --
How to hear the hungry-haunted clouds
  their ghosts in chimes and echoes

Flecks

Water always dreams remarkably at night --
    Stray lights puddle
        with steps into.
    What little moon there is
        is damply dressed.
    If wind comes up at all or forgets
        no matter --
            up-splashings still make
            our drousings wish.

And mud grins
    and shadows are
        our dearest friends
While coming ice (the best of fears) tings in.
    Somewhere near
        but just beyond
        our pillows flow.

Then fog fluffs up
    as tucks inspire
        our rustle-drips our murmurs
        our sleeping flecks --
            when silver skims
            the shiny dark.

In the Next Room Over

I'll bet you whatever you want
That she won't make it through the night
        and that's not being dreary
        that's just being honest

So anything out loud she says
        pay attention to
But especially do
        if you hear her coughing
        or if you smell doom in the hay
        or hear water gushing down drains
        because she's preparing

Trust me
Long long ago when things were as simple
        as that finger in your ear
She was a goddess
        like smoke is in fall
She was as pure as poured milk
            or the fullest of apples
That was then
Now the situation is a gaspy fish
        and the need to avoid and look away
        is deeply with us

But oh will you just look here at this little frame --
        There we were once
        posed under a tree
        lined up like sparrows
She was the robin

So I tell you this with my heart for my throat --
        a cool damp word is
        the least and most we can do for her now

Ferment

What if fruit got left out too long
      for love of course but better?

And what if cabbage was put down in jars as
      children grab swings
      but tart as well
      and lids at last?

What if summers all walked back in time
      like soured milk perhaps for years and years
      to froth?

And what if joy
      turned into this and more --
      as if worlds of fresh
      were made to change?

And opened crocks brewed such sour grins
      for peering in?

What if worlds were swirled around
      inside
With stirs and stirs
      so every spoon
      imagined wonders
      soon to be?

Foam

I got married to unclear a long while ago
    and have been faithful to my muddle ever since.
I remember the cloudy day we met
    and how my heart went blurry with love
    then or there.

At some point we started a family --
Our child was more of a windy tree than a person.
More like leaves rustling
    than a teen.
And like most parents
I don't understand but love our child wildly.

We also built a home back then
    that even now seems
    more of a lean-to --
A shifting spot that's barely balanced
    like a train's far-off whistle.

Who knows
    maybe we'll both live long enough
    me and my fuzzy
    to enjoy our silvery gold anniversary.
If so maybe we'll celebrate by taking a swim somewhere
    with water swirling over us.
What fun and how fitting a treat that would be --
    all tossed about
    in a foamy loving froth.

Any Moment Of

O for smooth and flow
    and bending towards

O for over climb
    those smells of green
        and eyes that whistle through

O for light and hearts
    their turning so
        to more and more

O for smooth or near
    on winds of where

And o for any moments of
    all silence said
    then ever on

O for thus until
    and more
    for every breath or stray

Murmur Worlds

If I opened with your eyes
    this morning's arms around me
What would soft sounds make and be
    all blurs that yawn with gazing

And if I whispered like your eyes
    those blinks to every always
How could daybreak over me
    such murmur worlds this early

If I held them while they rose --
    slept through your eyes
    then opened them
    the more

Or if now but then
    I was your eyes
    with morning's arms around me

Evening

Gnats know how lovely you are.
So do yucca whorls here on the island that makes you
      Takes you towards whispering clouds
      Takes you into rose-risks of sunshine
          and deep ferns peeled back
          to reveal those hiddens of you.

No one else but you goldens the gnats
      or walks up the sand
      shouldering the air
      like a country.

Bread in Hand

But even after all of this
    farmers keep farming
    for every one of us
They bend the sun
    and raise the earth
    each day for us
They round each rough
    and tamp down these fears
    for each of us
Yes after all of this
    they're the hope of life for us

And even after all of this
    the baggers stackers sorters drivers checkers
    field workers and grocery store sweepers too
    are here for us
Like bowls of life
    they give us each our every day
    and so renew that sense of trust for us

And even after all of this
    and just as much
    are those who volunteer to serve the soup
The ones who help and give and care
    on our behalf
Their hands and hearts
    shape our thanks --
No matter what else happens
    they are life itself for us

And yes even after all of this
These days seem like furrowed fields to us
    with darkest shadows across the view
    but also with
        rows on rows of green
        that grin wide and new

just like those who stand and wave
with bread in hand
for each of us
through all of this

Everif

There must be more mes somewhere --
    More twin trees out there waiting.

Maybe they wink in my dusty outskirts
    or maybe they're up some mountain's sloping shim
    or in gurgles I can hardly hear
    or maybe they're hidden deep in night time sighs
    or inside my shy downside throaty love
        of pockets.

I don't know but
    there has to be more than one of me
    more than just this single ruffled napkin
    over my cookie plate.
More mes than me
    who live by tucking in.

My others are probably where the dandles grin --
    they keep watching for
    keep waiting by
    on corners of
    in echoes from.

Like everknew or alwaysif
    like hung up socks or curving wings
My others live
    for windy days.

Rumbles

Easy sigh me
    Hum away my stumbling nights
    Calm my rustling
    Hush my eyes
    Drift my furrows

Easy sigh me
    Whisper back the shadows
    Pause my rumble
    Lull my whys
    Grin towards all the coming trouble

Easy sigh me
    Trace me with a touch that dreams
    Flicker away my dark
        with candle sake
    And then with that
    Window me the morning

Smart Dumb

She was born inside out
    the size of a heavy orange.
And the story goes that she was wobbly from the very start.
Even as a little girl
    she was so smart and so damn dumb together --
    that's the way sometimes.

Well, wouldn't you know it,
    dead solved the problem.
The full story isn't important
    but what is is that at about nineteen or so
    she fell jaw drop in love
    with someone who just wouldn't, couldn't and didn't.
Someone, like too close to a fire --
    yes, with those kind of eyes.

And the thing was there was no warning her at all.
    Not any.

And oh my goodness
    the rumors were rich enough to live on.

But here's the thing really --
    She ended up like a tree toppled over
        with all her roots up in the air.
    Hers was a big sideways life
        that just never really got started.
    And of course, she's gone now but is wholly famous.

That's what starting out with too many wants
    will do in an all or nothing sort of way.

So, the lingery question is this --
    Is it truly best to leave nature alone,
        or to invite it in for a chat over dinner?

Over and Besides

Praise for all whims of curve
For arrivals' grins
For pures that bend
    and windows' ledgings

Praise in ways that lift
    through pockets' wings
Through ringing sprigs
    their beams of firsts
    those pink dirts of Spring
    or brimming

Praise with hearts that over and besides
    through wanders' turns
    towards loping hills and humming ears
    towards hopes and on

Praise for most and deep inside --
    what curls with tinge
    or jumps the flowing

Curly Heart

What were he
    to always me
        of can't this won't
    this such of me
        with lose don't so
    but glory too my curly heart?

What were he
    to why I did
    or cotton in
        such shirts and wind
    the all of me and up
    of wishing why?

What were he in this --
    to go me
    to for me
    or scribbled me
    the want?

Where You Are

This crumble-cake of hope
This held up high tray of joy
This down deep sparkled flute
This allelu
This opened fizz in-waiting
This broom up-kick and views --
          the wonders
Yes, this ever-elfin jiggle dance
This zinnia burst and brightly led
This ribbony glory
This harking gurgle
This wiggle popping muddy lope.

Gathered Gate

Where crackles on every fence's limb
    twitch with bird-breast swell
    and flounce to full
    on crossbeams.

Where gathered gates are thrilled above
    as swirls and nestlings chime
    to rounder fields with rotting joys of windy rhymes
    in garish notes like perched songs flung.

Where crazed with every latch of paint --
    this Spring
        these Sarahs and these Sams
        in worlds of wet and brings and give
    to every flapping laundry leg.

Or hammer's ping like day-struck sights
    each mowed each row
    and tasted sun these weedlets cling.

This finally swung-out open swoop
    the teasing pink of stems
        that hover gully pools
        as wanting will
        or could be does
        and always has.

Where asks of wise and patch and breeze
    are made of daying wings.

Muddy

I wish I could tell which of my friends
  will be friends forever
  and who will just walk off whistling into the woods.

Which ones I wonder will chance choose
  for keeps
  from the randoms?

So many slip away without saying much
  and others drop off when I throw a fit
  and some turn sour
   soon after ripening.

Walls tall as sixty-five
  also make it harder
  to keep in touch.

The starts and stops of friendship are muddy mysteries.

So I guess that there's no way to predict
  who will end up being there
   after all
   waving the checkered flag
   and grinning.

Spoons or Rakes

What we so need now
    is glow --

The sort of night that embers make
The sounds in nests
    or apples' shapes

We need the kind of spoons or rakes
    that neighbors love

Or hailing lights on distant shores
    that warm the boats

A glow that gives more than it takes

We need the wool of early years
    or more
What holds us close when
    nothing's near

Touching Up

No matter what I do
I always miss a spot or two
      and while I don't recall her whisper now
I tend to when
      touching up

I've often splotched the dripping downs --
Orange beams her sounds
Those found of founds --
      my mother's winking chin
      so full of
      nodding and surround

Me that lucky dip-brush kid
The whitewashed barn I did back then
      in skies of lakes and reds --
          my sloshing can of dreams

And all she said to me --
         in stirs or mixed or nearly dones --
           by holding

Gush

For garden hoses' flow
     and a whistle's run
     from here to there

How clouds push blue
     through wide-open doors

Or when fences over-bloom
     and finding never ends

And for color's sound and evening's strum --
     that push
     that grateful
        give and give of gush

Yes and for this spin of course
     of cups and plates and cake
     before guests come

Soup to Nuts

The crowd shrank like zip
The room suddenly became just you
    to me
All background noise crumpled
Even the air
    swept its hair back

And all of my eyes
    head to toes
    soup to nuts
    in be-bad holy light
      zoomed in
      and nothing else even twitched

Then and there
    I got dug up like civilizations
    like age stampeded

And every squeak of melting ice
Every clumsy clink of sip
Every bit of my fizz
Coughed and swore
    with swigging.

Mud Ajar

Love hay as daybreaks toss
    and fill full-barrows
    with allelu
Push pull soggy meadows
    to hallow be

Green or boots high raise the low
    to allelu
Beckon find the ditches
    or blend these clouds
    as firsts of all

For mud ajar
For breakfast fields and feast
    of heaven-takes
Where planks sing-swing
    to allelu

Here where beaks are barns
    that loop through when
    as rain lifts praise
    on trill of rakes

Listened Twigs

These trees a choir
  in early fine
  their waking limbs
When snowflakes hear within themselves
  of how beginning sounds

These few steps down
  as up above
  what crows inspire
  their calls to towards
  or fars abound

And trees their choir
  this opened view
  as reaching out
  when clouds unbound

Hear frost as flight
  slips in-between
  whatever sings

The browns of whispered green
These lyric twigs
  in listening light

Ancient

What a pyramid this life is --

    my wife, my driveway, my nephew,
piled on top of my hat, my illness, my hobby,
    my town, my clocks, my husband, my lamp,
just above my fence and
the fields beyond,
then higher still
    my lungs, my ego, my age, my cusp,
    my tattoos, my grannies, my snacks

What a stack of rocks all of this has become
    with sand everywhere
    and camels chewing straw
    in the foreground

Open

On thresholds make this new
    and door wide these discoveries
Swing full-flying open --
    awakened to and rising from
    a gate-lucky song

And beyond these coulds and maybes
    with every patch of weeds or loose
    in all of sprouting
Wonder as whatever sings

Then fold this view
    inside those wings

Yes perch on leafy light or stems
    like bluebirds
    made of handsome

Prancing

Grackle me
     these slick-spots.

Trash toss me with squawking
     and puddle my wet black colors flecked
     or muddy eyes my feet.

Then gutter my branches more
     and peck at whatever's less of.

Or flock to where
     soggy flicks
     in clouds that thin and flee.

All to make a show of perky charms --
     my cackle-call that's flouncing.

Sign a Lease

When praise slips quietly by
    dig a hole
When feet swell
    wave hello
When the skies boil or bloom
    go sweep the stoop
When gears slip
    comb hair
When children grow up
    count to ten.

Chairs

Like you
I am whoever
　　loses clouds
　　or sits on branches

I am why oh why hollow
　　and like you
　　have questions that echo
　　and crack

I am knotty trunks for no reason
　　or beetles boring bark
　　or chirps malarkey

And like you
　　I start at rot
　　to find woody love
　　that wanders

Then I end up where I become
　　forest duff like you
　　or moss loving what's skyward

When More

What should you do
When bad gathers around to squawk
When fog snakes in
    or ledges creak and crack

What can you do to ward off
    or hold tight
    or wait out

What's there to do when all the world votes no
    or cuts off escapes
    or growls like beware

What's left to do
When more just isn't enough
When apples bite back
Or shadows turn off the lights

Open For

If time is gone
Then where am I --
Still ready for
But nubby winged

If time is gone
Then how to start
And how to treat my heart
That faintly feels
Some sting and buzz

If time is gone
Then how will hills
Hailed in newest greens
Bring skies inside my hollow branch

If time has gone and left behind
Then how to further on --
Like days curved up to clouds
Like swarms that feel fall coming.

Day-glow

God is inside splinters
And whenever floors creak or crack
    that's a glory divine indeed
Yes the archangel of whatever's broken
    transfigures wings --
In fact what powers the piddly or punctured
    is simply sublime.

And when God asks why or what
    that's when tree rot begins
Or in a hoodie
    cups a match --
It's in that flash
    there's sainthood --
What miraculous leakage!

So watch out
    because if the Devil then
    says *phooey* --
Just like that
    our every high-road cause
    will veer off in the fog
        towards fail
        towards day-glow cones
        that are all lined up
        like a hell-hot snaking tail.

Inside

Grass is as gay
>as left-open gates
>or arms stretched wide. His.
And whenever water gurgles over rocks
>that's gay as well.
Or think of shirts that let sun in.
>In the back. Him.

Clouds can be very gay, too, backlit.
And so are starlings
>peppery up in that tree. So him.

They are all almost as gay as railroad tracks at dusk
>or fading whistles.
Almost as gay as grinning fields inside of eyes.

The first time that I felt what was supposed to be
>was in a field. His.
>When time suddenly seemed too grateful.
When all the suns became wholly new --
>It was a very inside outside and
>wondrous thing. Him.
And after that I never seemed to stretch or even whistle
>or roll up my sleeves
>or share a sandwich
>>in the same way.

Losing Birthdays

One of my grandmothers grew
        deep-red geraniums on her front porch
        for everyone strolling by in the summer
        to admire
My other grandmother
        trained a rosebush of palest pinks
        and heavenly scent
        up over her back door
            I was lost

And so
        there is how just now
        these fields of sunrise
        forget such birthdays
While blackbirds pick and pick
        and ticks climb up

What good am I
        at taking such things inside
These deepest loves and smallest sounds

And I've been told that
        wherever he went my imaginary uncle
        caused people to shyly grin
He was strange they all said
But people loved him anyway
        for his dreamy ways

He was just like Johnny Appleseed who
        I still believe
        dropped barefoot seeds
        on every spot
            that could be found
            poor or steep
            year by year
            from here to then

Dewest Prowl

Inside a boy's new spigot
    within his barking heart
Among a boy's tufts of spy
    or hillsides' clamored sack
    his strides of why
    and wings that wide
    or clouds for blue

Before a boy's then but now
    in weeds of dewest prowl
Between his sudden founds
    and clues
    or panting sprigs of who to be --
    this wispy kid of man

These curls that scruff
    the dripping years
These wanderings out
    to what towards when

And how he'll bring back home
    each slanting grin
        found in fields or dares
        as if brand new

This Where

The shades in hymns I've always heard
    or rakes that pull my heart

The roots I sing inside myself
    I've always longed to be

The leaning sheds that are my life

The straw I've gathered round
    to family forth
    and all these wings that marry me

They carry me
    to out beyond
    to fields of who I'll see

Conjure

Pretend that there's a tune inside this line
Pretend there's a wide-open humming window right here
       or a whistle that's weaving in and out
       of each of these written trees --
              those kind of sounds

Imagine that there's a rain-drip background to these words
       the springtime kind that must be touched
       yes
       with colors humming the pages' corners
              Imagine that

Or conjure all of this
       while recalling the swelling of a storm
       where up and down collide with hay
              in thundered vistas made of rhyme

With such fields of make in mind
              or jottings down
       imagine if all of this was whimmed away
           as weeds that hum
           as poem-cakes --
              their candles

Valentine

And up is low
And famished full
And night is day in many ways
And hardly if is really so

And love stays still and strays
And summer shivers slow
And inside's out
And up is low
And high soars down

Flinch

The world is full of skills
And knowings of
    yes
    but wide eyes are wiser than
    any teacher

Too bad in fact
    that books aren't made by swerving off
Too bad such smarts hate bursts
        or bangs
        because flinch is where
        the weather's made

Flinch is really where we feel akin
    (ask any cringe)

And flinch is how
    the blare of sirens really teach
    or more badly said
How guessing knows.

Little Else

Cold's green is the finest thing
    especially when mornings seem
    too all and few.

When snow is barely on
    first green --
        those sudden-seens
        song wantings.

Newest green with yellow hope
    that's deeply in
Where wantings grow --
    those sprouting chills of yearning.

And birds are all upside down
    as meltings cling
To barely green that stays
    unlasting.

How newness sings to little else.

Such shyness in the finest green --
    faint sun a spark
    mud's splatter.

After All

For some reason
      you think in a different way when
            you go outside.
It doesn't make any difference
      if you're in the city
            or far up in the hills.
It doesn't matter if there is time or not
      or if it's spring or fall
            or what you've had to eat.

When you step outside from being in
      even for just a minute
      you think of bigger things
      like how to convince someone of what's important
            after they're gone
      or how to get to three hundred years from now
            by hitchhiking
      or no matter what kind of moon's up there
            how you should strive to become
            more and more like butter.

Ages Ears

Oh my friends of all we may
     this wonder seems
     so colors wishing eye-ward

And oh my friends as if we could
     to ever blessed such sounds
     of where to when
     of seedling dreams
     we and grateful

My friends and oh as if we surely must
     amazement here
     and living in
     with what may be
     with vast to do

This now my friends and why
     and oh and how
     such apple sacks that give us

These ages ears --
     our oh in telling others
     of this where and more
     these listening founds
     for fulling

Uphill

If asked
    what the most beautiful sight
    on earth is
I'd probably say
    that it's the feeling
    of a blanket half covering bare shoulders in Spring
    with a drizzling rain outside --
That is surely one of the most important loves
    to live through

I think I'd also have to say
    that whatever I don't understand
Is really lovely in the hungriest sort of way
    because it makes me pedal uphill
    especially for the kind of soup or bread
    I've come to crave

And to be honest
    I'd also have to admit
    what I've known all along --
That for something to really float or glow
    or leave love in me
It has to be
    out of place
    in an understood-only-afterwards
    sort of way.

Pretty Boy Floyd

Erase everything that you may know about him
His place of birth
      or age
      or even how he died
            in a spray of bullets
Ignore all of that
It makes no difference
He hardly made a difference
Except my goodness his name

No matter what you may think about him
      there's his nickname --
Somehow it brings to mind farmers
      especially beet or wheat farmers
      in bowls of dust
Farmers who shook their heads at that name
      or wiped their noses and grinned

A name from so outside the Midwest and yet
      so inside it --
            a blue-ribbon jar of pickles
            or chrome fenders
Floyd -- meaning an uncle or post office clerk
But also Pretty Boy --
      meaning a curl of cigarette smoke
      or cream-colored suspenders
      or even a French postcard

Nothing that went wrong with him counts much now
But just like with Bonnie Prince Charlie
We want to see his picture anyway
And when we finally do
      framed in a very different world
      we whisper *good gracious* to ourselves.

Back to Me

If only I could go back somehow
    to those colors that evening --
They would look at me now
    even from their ways-away
    and recall all of my trying

What would I remember --
    the touch of what I couldn't say
    the sounds I've always wanted
    or the maps left unopened

What's hard is turning away this time
    trying to reach some blue or path or rhyme
    this once --
        The views beyond adoring.

Chanted

Day-make candles grin anew
    as almost firstings light
Their flicker hearts these swaying lifts --
    our telling lives our yellow-glows
    and ages gone or wonders new
Like foliage or a morning's chin

How dawn-most candles best the Spring --
    For chanted vines that bring
        up-twines inside
    For such and all of these
        our flowsome days of make

Give or Gots

These greetings from --
Laundry flung as love on gates
And buckets pail the morning's wet
     or chores slung and shoulder spades
     while pies to sills their slatted beams
Or branches' shady-seeped
     where honest dreams

These days that keep --
Dug up or burrowed through
     each weedy fence
And seeds of fare-thee-well
Or start of hearts that rabbits bring
     or folds in wind
     aloud as skies

Our opened eyes from here to there --
     these give or gots
     new knowing

Succotash

My country so Polly
So jack of all trades
    and confetti
This yard sale of nations
    with ditches of weeds
    and cornfields split open
The tar in my whistles

My country the talons
    and scars after oozing

The sparklers my country that wake up
    but ransack what happened
        and broad beans that dazzle the mud

My country all arrows shot heaven
    with swearing

My country in sparrows
    gone haywire and hobo
The screen doors to wisdom
    slammed shut and gone off to
    with maps left behind

My country these blackboards of silence
    and mis-spells
My country my country
    so flies over pie

Clustered

You peach the days
    and make more wheres
    to roam in
You orchard through
    with whistling seeds or baskets
A damping of branches --
    towards paths of ripened clings above
    those whispered leaves
    or rows of distance
    rambling

You peach the days
    and grateful every beam
Your harvest shimmers the sun
    as weeds do
    in shade surround
Through sap or wings or blurry juice
    their tangles

What sweeter is this reaching for --
    this found to be
    in clusters.

In-Waiting

When I speak twig
    above me
    the sounds are unimaginable
Each swollen bud laces its shoes
    and those earwigs their pinches
    squeak out to my growing
        gold days
They grab my damp heart in-waiting

And when I see such tremendous
    shake-salting importance on bird tails
    or feel a will that won't that matters
    it's then from roofs atop me
        that sudden notions wing me
        towards how to live

When I turn into twigs now
    my sap dives deeper
    and the claps
        clap louder --
        up to those winking drip-song
        wisely eaves

Ripened Brooms

To search for home this pollened ground
    where wide as shoulders
    or days become
    and golden roves
    the gold that's found
This ponded sheen and home within
    with doors that hover

To come meadowed towards luster's swill
    or Autumn's climb
    or cherished brooms
Their tousled lift
    from ripened this and all around

To slant alive
    towards where and roam

How yellow dust is wings their years
    and welcomes such
    these grasses' sounds --
    this much to more

Of all that's found
    what lasts beyond --
These blowing birds
    the seeds of home

Gift of Guess

How fog comes towards
        the newness in our older days
        the blue inside of gray
        or spidered doors

And leaves
        leave their sounds as true
            as browns beneath
        or stones their damp
        or lamps switched on

Then too what dusk does well
        or onion skins
        or tree-rot steam

How such crinkled light
        makes all the crows
        their evenings

Or how the musty years
        in grapes that hang
        or wasps or carried pails
        and fielded ways
        come in between --

This gift of guess
        on shelves of webs
        in jars of nails

Tin Roof

When I was 17
    apples were busheled in baskets --
    and I was the straw under all of those
        red round spirits.
All the light coming through
    the shed's planks
    was slanted across them
    and every wasp in the world
    hovered just above them.
    Yes
Whatever apples were
    I wanted to be.

    And in a way
When I was 17
    apples ate me --
What was to become my heart
    was really some wild weedy patch
    in the orchard back then.
And any sheen reflecting off their skins
    or the barn's tin roof
    was all that I wanted to be.

When I was 17
    with every seed buried deep inside
    even my gangly gaze was humming.
And somehow I knew before tasting anything
    tartly sweet
    that that was what I wanted to be
    right there
    in the baskets.

This If

I fly myself
 far as can be
 like windows do or
 doors beyond
This reaching sky
 these trees
 of all that's gone
Or coming to
 and rounded beams

I fly as how
 open is
And porches swing
 up to towards
 each rhyme undone
 to tell of fill and full
 where blue is now

I fly this if
 but also more
Where clouds love rakes
 or fields are curls
 to forever where
Or haloes fling
 my scattered firsts --
 this day that rings

Acknowledgements

Many of the poems in this collection were written, with rake on shoulder, during the 2020-21 pandemic. A few, including *Ode to the Edge* and *An Gorta Mór*, were written during a residency at the Heinrich Böll Writers Cottage on Achill Island, Co. Mayo, Ireland. I thank those who helped with the manuscript including my sisters, Jane and Elizabeth. I'm grateful, too, to the Atmosphere Press team. I also thank editors of the indicated journals or collections for publishing versions of the following poems.

Achill Sound – Words for the Wild, The Echo World, A New Ulster, 2019 Bridgewater Anthology, Verse Virtual
After All – Headstuff
An Gorta Mór – Welter
Ancient – Ginosko
Any Moment Of – Flapper Press
Back to Me – Contemporary American Voices
Bread in Hand – Poetry X Hunger, In the Midst – A COVID Anthology
Chanted – Alexandria Quarterly, The Write Blend
Clatter – 21st Century Flow
Conjure – Oyster River Pages
Curly Heart – Brave New World Magazine
Day-glow – Better than Starbucks
Evening – The Write Blend
Everif – Backbone Mountain Review, The Write Blend
Ferment – Flapper Press
Flecks – The Write Blend
Flinch – The Short of It
Foam – The Write Blend
Gathered Gate – Poetry Kit's Year of the Plague Anthology
Gift of Guess – Ponder Savant
Gush – Thieving Magpie
Inside – The Remnant Archive
In the Next Room Over – Hedge Apple
In-Waiting – Thieving Magpie

Listened Twigs (published as Listened Branches) – Thieving
    Magpie
Losing Birthdays – West Trade Review
Magic – Orbis
Muddy – A New Ulster
Mud Ajar – Ginosko
Ode to the Edge – Words for the Wild, The Write Blend
Open – Ginosko
Open For – Affinity CoLab
Our Us – Words for the Wild
Over and Besides – Clementine Unbound
Patio – A New Ulster
Prancing – Thin Air Online
Pretty Boy Floyd – Poetry South
Radio – Hedge Apple
Rumbles – River and South Review
Sign a Lease – Ginosko
Since – HoCoPoLitSo's Blossoms of Hope
Smart Dumb – vox poetica
So What – vox poetica
Soup to Nuts – Affinity CoLab
Spoons or Rakes – North of Oxford's Pandemic Poetry, Mike
    Maggio's Pandemic Poetry, DC Trending, Frank Kelso
    Wolfe's Memorial Page
Quiets Come – Ponder Savant and Fine Lines
This Where – West Trade Review
Tin Roof – North of Oxford, 2019 Bridgewater Anthology,
    Studio B's Superheroes
Touching Up – Skylight Kicker and on Facebook
Uphill – Clock Radio Magazine
Valentine – The Short of It
When More – Better than Starbucks, Frank Kelso Wolfe's
    Memorial page
Where You Are – Brave New World Magazine, Affinity
    CoLab

About Atmosphere Press

Atmosphere Press is an independent, full-service publisher for excellent books in all genres and for all audiences. Learn more about what we do at atmospherepress.com.

We encourage you to check out some of Atmosphere's latest releases, which are available at Amazon.com and via order from your local bookstore.